FESTIVAL FUN
for the Early Years

HANUKKAH
and
ROSH HASHANA

- **Fun activity ideas** -
- **Photocopiable resources** -
- **Information on customs and beliefs** -

D0452554

SCHOLASTIC   **Linda Mort**

CREDITS

Author
Linda Mort

Editor
Susan Howard

Assistant Editor
Jennifer Shiels

Series Designer
Catherine Mason

Designer
Andrea Lewis

Cover Illustration
Catherine Mason

Illustrations
Sarah Warburton

Text © Linda Mort 2004
© 2004 Scholastic Ltd

Designed using Adobe InDesign

Published by Scholastic Ltd
Villiers House
Clarendon Avenue
Leamington Spa
Warwickshire
CV32 5PR

www.scholastic.co.uk

Printed by Bell & Bain Ltd, Glasgow

3 4 5 6 7 8 9   6 7 8 9 0 1 2 3

British Library Cataloguing-in-Publication Data
A catalogue record for this book is available from the British Library.

ISBN 0-439-97153-5

CONTENTS

 HANUKKAH

 ROSH HASHANA

INTRODUCTION

Celebrating festivals with young children

Young children find it easier to take in new information about a festival if they can relate it to their own experiences. When discussing Hanukkah or Rosh Hashana traditions and celebrations, you could talk about buying new clothes for special occasions, eating party food, attending a place of worship, and dancing. If you have one or more children in your group who celebrate the festival concerned, ask them to tell you how they prepare for and celebrate the festival. You can ask family members for more details.

Present the information in a way that the children can understand by telling it in the form of a story. If you do not have any children who celebrate the festival in your group, you could hold up two pictures of a girl and a boy cut from magazines. Give the children names and say that they are, for example, Jewish. Describe some everyday details about each child such as the patterns on their socks and their favourite toys, then go on to describe how they prepare for the festival and celebrate it. Invite the children to add their own comments and experiences that they have in common with the two children. When you tell any festival story, explain that the girl and boy listened to this story, too.

Multicultural awareness

Give the children first-hand experiences of the items and customs of the festival that you are celebrating, by setting up your home corner to represent a decorated home. Ask parents, community members or religious centres to lend you items. If possible, arrange for groups of children to go shopping for relevant items from ethnic shops, or buy them from educational suppliers (see 'Resources' on page 48). Occasionally eat 'festival' food, not only at the time of the festival but also at other times of the year.

Involving parents and the community

If possible, ask families to send in photographs or short home videos of their festival celebrations. Invite parents into your setting to talk about how they celebrate festivals in their homes and to demonstrate some typical festival cookery ideas. Encourage grandparents to visit too, explaining how the celebration of the festival may have changed over time, or comparing celebrations in other countries. If possible, arrange a visit to a nearby place of worship, such as a synagogue.

How to use this book

This book covers the festivals of Hanukkah and Rosh Hashana. For each festival, there is a section of background information and a full-colour poster with suggestions for its use. There is the traditional story associated with each festival, as well as six pages of cross-curricular ideas, plus songs, rhymes and photocopiable activities. The 'Festival planner' topic web shows how the cross-curricular ideas link to the six Areas of Learning. In addition, for each festival, there are six further ideas focusing on craft and gift ideas, cookery, display, role-play, dance and 'Hold your own celebration'.

BACKGROUND INFORMATION AND PLANNING

Dates
● Hanukkah (with the 'H' pronounced as a 'ch' sound, as in the Scottish word 'loch') is known as the Jewish Festival of Light. The festival lasts for eight days.
● The first day of Hanukkah falls on the following dates during the next three years:
    8 December 2004 (Jewish Year 5765)
    26 December 2005 (Jewish Year 5766)
    16 December 2006 (Jewish Year 5767).
● The festival begins at sunset on the day before the first dates shown above. This is when the first candle is lit (see below). Dates beyond 2006 can be found on the website: www.jewishpeople.net/jewishholidays.html

Religious beliefs
● Hanukkah, the Hebrew word for 'dedication', commemorates the relighting and re-dedication to God of the golden lamp in the Jerusalem temple in 165 BC, after a period of oppression of the Jewish people by the Syrian-Greek king Antiochus. Jews were not allowed to pray to God or lead a Jewish way of life. Greek idols were placed in the temple, and Jews were ordered to bow down to them. An old Jewish priest called Mattathias and his five sons, the bravest of whom was Judah, the 'Maccabee' (Hebrew for 'hammer'), resisted, and gathered a small army. They lived in the hills and caves outside Jerusalem. After Mattathias' death, Judah became leader of the 'Maccabees', who became so skilful at surprise attacks that, although greatly outnumbered, they eventually defeated Antiochus' army.

The Maccabees found the temple desecrated and began restoring it. They wanted to relight the golden lamp, the Menorah, but there remained only one small container of oil, just enough to burn for one day. With no other choice, the Maccabees lit the oil. Miraculously, the Menorah stayed alight for eight days – enough time for new oil to be produced.
● After that, Jewish families began to commemorate the event by lighting a special Hanukkah Menorah, called a Hanukiah. This has eight branches, and one extra for the 'shammash' (servant) candle, used to light the others.
● The candles are lit on eight successive nights; one on the first night, two on the second and so on. The festival celebrates the Jewish people's faith in God, which brought about the victory over Antiochus, the miracle of the oil and the survival of the Jewish religion and culture when threatened with extinction.

Customs and traditions
● The customary greeting at Hanukkah is 'Chag sameach' (the 'ch' pronounced as in the Scottish 'loch', and the 'e' pronounced as an 'eh' sound). This means 'happy festival'.
● To celebrate the festival, people eat food that has been cooked in oil. This commemorates the miracle of the oil.

• Children celebrate the festival by receiving gifts and playing the 'driedel' game. The driedel is a special Hanukkah spinning top.

• Hanukkah is celebrated in a festive atmosphere, in contrast to the solemnity of Rosh Hashana and Yom Kippur. It is customary to give children money – either real or chocolate – which is known as 'Hanukkah gelt'.

• Families give money to charity and also like to devise their own gift-giving customs.

Celebrations

• Families celebrate Hanukkah in their own homes by lighting the Hanukiah for eight nights. A blessing is recited before and after the lighting of the Hanukiah. After the blessing, children are given gifts and the family enjoys food which has been cooked in oil. Typical celebration food includes 'latkes' (grated potato cakes) or 'sufganiyot' (doughnuts).

• Children and adults enjoy sharing activities together, such as spinning the driedel or playing card games. Because the Syrian-Greeks prohibited the Jews from studying the Torah (the Jewish law), they did so in secret. According to tradition, if they were discovered, they would quickly substitute a driedel. Playing card games and games of chance also helped people to pass the long winter nights.

• Hanukkah parties are held for children, when they play team action games and enjoy Israeli dancing. The parties take place in the home or at synagogue religion schools.

• During the festival, Hanukiot (plural) are also lit in synagogues, just before the start of normal services.

Things to remember

• Unlike Rosh Hashana and Yom Kippur, which are known as 'High Holy Days' when people are not permitted to work, during Hanukkah people may work during the day and celebrate the festival in the evening.

• People are not allowed to use the light of a Hanukiah for illumination, or for working or reading.

• It is customary for the same 'shammash' candle to be used for the duration of the festival. The 'shammash' is extinguished and saved after use on each night.

• On a Hanukiah, the candle-holder for the 'shammash' should be raised above the others. Candles are placed in the candle-holders in a right to left direction, but are lit from left to right.

Using the poster

Display the poster and point to the Star of David in the centre of the Hanukiah. Explain to the children that the pictured 'shammash' candle is a new one, but that some people like to use the same one, all through the eight nights, blowing it out each time, so that by the eighth night it is quite small. Talk about how most Hanukiot, like the one shown in the poster, are made of metal such as brass or silver, because metal will not catch fire and will not break when the melted wax is scraped off each evening, after the candles have burned out.

HANUKKAH
FESTIVAL PLANNER

CROSS-CURRICULAR IDEAS

Personal, social and emotional development

Early Learning Goal — Have a developing awareness of their own needs, views and feelings and be sensitive to the needs, views and feelings of others.

Talk About — Tell the children that, at Hanukkah, some families like to give 'special gifts' that do not involve buying an object. Encourage them to think of some special gifts that they could give for free, such as a big cuddle.

Early Learning Goal — Consider the consequences of their words and actions for themselves and others.

Talk About — Explain that when the Maccabees first went to live in the caves, they were probably a little afraid of the dark. To help them feel better, they talked to each other and soon understood that there was nothing to be afraid of.

Further Ideas

● Talk about times when the Maccabees would have felt sad, tired, surprised and happy. Draw each 'expression' and stick them on to alternate sections of an upturned umbrella to make a giant driedel. Take turns to spin it and, depending on the expression on which it falls, talk about what makes you feel sad, tired, surprised or happy.

● Explain that it was a 'very happy surprise' when the Maccabees realised that the oil had lasted for eight days. Encourage the children to discuss happy surprises such as rainbows, snow or seeing a baby walk for the first time.

EIGHT SPECIAL GIFTS

What you need
The rhyme 'Eight special gifts' on page 21.

What to do
● Read the rhyme together with the children. Discuss how at Hanukkah, families like to give out special gifts to show that they care.
● Talk about the different things mentioned in the verses. Invite the children to suggest other special things that they can do to show that they care.
● Encourage the children to make up their own actions to the rhyme. Once they are confident, invite parents to watch as you recite it all the way through.

DON'T BE AFRAID!

What you need
Shoebox, covered inside and out with black paper; dolls' house bed; play person to go in the bed under a paper 'blanket' (see illustration).

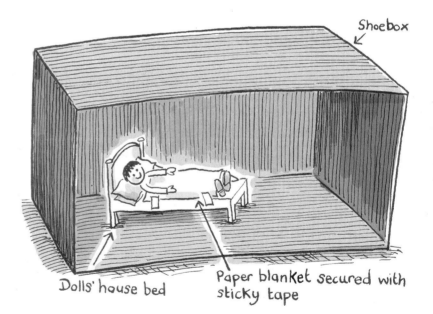

Shoebox

Dolls' house bed

Paper blanket secured with sticky tape

What to do
● Sit together in a circle and discuss how the Maccabees would have felt when they first went into the caves. Put the play person in the bed into the shoebox. Explain that the play person is a little afraid of the dark in their 'bedroom'.
● Pass the 'bedroom' around the circle, and ask everyone to peep inside and say something to help the play person stop feeling afraid.

Communication, language and literacy

WORD DANCE

Early Learning Goal
Extend their vocabulary, exploring the meanings and sounds of new words.

Talk About
At the end of the game, read and talk about each word together.

What you need
Eight household candles on a tray; 12 play bricks; eight yellow paper 'flames'; eight pieces of white paper (each 30cm by 10cm); felt-tipped pen; CD or tape of lively music; music-playing facilities.

What to do
● Write each of the following words on to a piece of white paper: 'Hanukiah', 'Maccabees', 'festival', 'driedel', 'latkes', 'oil', 'fry' and 'sizzle'.
● Arrange the play bricks on the floor to make a Hanukiah.
● Hold up and read the words to a group of eight children.
● Give everyone a word, then ask the children to skip around the Hanukiah to the music.

● Stop the music and call out a word.
● Whoever has that word should place a candle on the Hanukiah, with their word above it, starting on the right-hand side.
● When all of the candles are positioned, ask everyone to count as you put a 'flame' above each candle, in a left-to-right direction.

COME TO THE PARTY!

Early Learning Goal
Write their own names and other things such as labels and captions and begin to form simple sentences, sometimes using punctuation.

Talk About
Tell the children that Hanukkah parties are held in synagogues and in people's homes. Has anyone ever visited a synagogue? Invite the children to share their experiences.

What you need
For a pair of children: two copies of 'Come to the party' photocopiable sheet on page 23; name card for each child; felt-tipped pens.

What to do
● Sit the children side by side and explain that they are going to write invitations to each other.
● Help one child trace over the letters on their name card with their index finger. Encourage them to verbalise the letter direction, for example, 'down, up and round'.
● Help the child to copy or overwrite their name underneath 'Love from...' on the photocopiable sheet. Repeat this with the second child.

● Ask the second child to 'teach' the first child, in your presence, how to write the second child's name underneath 'Invitation to...' on the first child's sheet. Encourage them to verbalise the letter direction.
● Repeat with the first child.

Further Ideas
● Write each of the following words on separate pieces of card: 'We', 'light', 'candles', 'We', 'spin', 'driedels', 'We', 'eat' and 'latkes'. Jumble up the words on the carpet, and challenge pairs of children to sort them out.
● Record 'The story of Hanukkah' on page 20 (or your own version) on to a tape for individual children to listen to, using headphones. Ask the children to make an illustrated concertina book to accompany it.

Mathematical development

Early Learning Goal Use language such as 'more' or 'less' to compare two numbers.

Talk About Tell the children that people enjoyed making up card games at Hanukkah, to help pass the long winter nights.

MACCABEE!

What you need
Two pieces of A4 card; scissors; felt-tipped pens.

What to do
● Cut each piece of card into quarters to make eight cards.
● Draw a black Hanukiah on each one, with a red 'shammash' candle in the centre.
● Draw two candles (starting from the right) on each Hanukiah of the first pair of cards.
● Draw three candles on each of the next two cards.
● Draw four candles and then five candles on the remaining pairs of cards.
● Let two children play a version of 'Snap!', saying 'Maccabee!' when they spot two Hanukiot with the same number of candles.
● Make the game more challenging by drawing the candles in different colours, so that the children have to look carefully to match the number of candles, irrespective of colour.

DRIEDEL FUN

Early Learning Goal In practical activities and discussion begin to use the vocabulary involved in adding and subtracting.

Talk About Show the children a real driedel, if possible, or the illustration on the photocopiable sheet on page 24. Explain that each of the four Hebrew letters is also the first letter of a word in the Hebrew saying, 'nes (miracle) gadol (great) hayah (happened) sham (there)', which means 'a great miracle happened there'.

What you need
Driedel, if possible (available from synagogues and RE resource suppliers such as TTS, see 'Resources' on page 48); if a driedel is not available, use 'Driedel fun' photocopiable sheet on page 24; square of card (10cm by 10cm); glue; glue spreader; awl (adult use); used matchstick; 40 counting cubes.

What to do
● Follow the instructions on photocopiable sheet to make a driedel.
● Working with a group of four children, give each child ten cubes.
● Ask everyone to put one cube into the 'kitty'.
● In turn, spin the driedel and follow the instructions to take or put back the cubes.
● After five minutes, stop playing and count up the cubes. Whoever has the most is the winner.

Further Ideas
● Using straws for candles, see if the children can work out how many candles would be needed for the eight nights of Hanukkah, including one 'shammash' candle. (They would need 37 in total.)
● Tie five short pieces of string on to five pieces of yellow sponge. Put them in a frying pan and recite 'Five jumping latkes', as in the rhyme 'Five fat sausages'. On the word 'bang!' let a child make a latke 'jump' out of the pan. Count how many are left each time.
● Buy a large bag of potatoes and encourage the children to line them up in size order.

HANUKKAH
CROSS-CURRICULAR IDEAS

LET'S FIND OUT

Early Learning Goal Begin to know about their own cultures and beliefs and those of other people.

What you need
'Let's find out' photocopiable sheet on page 25; Jewish artefacts (available from RE resource suppliers such as TTS, see 'Resources' on page 48); books about the Jewish religion (see 'Resources' on page 48).

Talk About Encourage the children to talk about other Jewish festivals that they may know about, such as Passover and Purim.

What to do
● Tell the children that Hanukkah is a festival that is celebrated by Jewish people.
● Let everyone examine and talk about the artefacts (if available) and find pictures of them in books.
● Talk about the pictures on the photocopiable sheet. Explain that the Star of David symbol appears on the flag of Israel, where many Jewish people live, and that they speak the Hebrew language.

● Tell the children that part of the Jewish Bible is called the Torah, which is written in Hebrew on scrolls.
● Explain that Jewish people pray to God in a synagogue, and that Jewish boys and men wear a 'kippah' (skullcap).
● Give each child a copy of the photocopiable sheet and encourage them to complete it, reminding them to look for the initial letter of the words as a clue.

WHAT SHALL WE USE?

Early Learning Goal Ask questions about why things happen and how things work.

What you need
Cleaning items, such as a real or toy vacuum cleaner, bath sponge and feather duster; the song 'What shall we use?' on page 21.

Talk About Tell the children that the Maccabees would not have been able to turn on taps for hot water. What might they have done instead?

What to do
● Talk about the cleaning problems that the Maccabees might have dealt with in the temple. What might they have used to clean up with?
● Invite the children to discuss how we clean today. What cleaning equipment and products do we use?
● Hold up and talk about the cleaning items, then invite everyone to join in with the words and actions to the song.

Further Ideas ● Explain that the temple lamp – the Menorah – would have been filled and lit with olive oil. Encourage the children to look at, smell, taste and touch a variety of olives, squeezing them to see the oil oozing out. Let everyone see and smell a bottle of olive oil.
● Let the children investigate 'spinners' and make a display. You could include a driedel, a spinning-top toy, a card disc on a string, a whip and top toy, and a gyroscope.

CROSS-CURRICULAR IDEAS

Physical development

AS STILL AS CAN BE

What you need
Eight small beanbags.

What to do
- Encourage one child to stand in front of a group of eight children.
- Ask the child to be a 'Hanukiah' and to stand with their arms stretched out. Explain that their head is the 'shammash'.
- Ask each child in the group to carefully place a small beanbag 'candle' on the arms of the 'Hanukiah' child (four on each) without them falling off.
- Increase the challenge by inviting the children to use other items, such as small plastic cups.

THE CANDLE CREW

What you need
Nine sand-play buckets filled with damp sand; one play brick; nine household candles; triangle and beater.

What to do
- Build a 'Hanukiah' with the buckets and play brick (see illustration).

- Put one candle – the shammash – in the bucket on the play brick.
- Ask seven children to sit on the floor, each holding a candle.
- Tap one child on the shoulder and ask them to move quickly and carefully, without bumping into anyone, and put their candle in the first bucket 'candleholder' on the right-hand side of the 'Hanukiah'.
- Ask the child to walk back quickly, touching someone else on the shoulder as they pass to signal that they can go, and so on.
- Challenge the group to fill the 'Hanukiah' before you play one note on the triangle.

Early Learning Goal
Move with control and co-ordination.

Talk About
Tell the children that it is very important that lighted candles do not fall out of a Hanukiah. Demonstrate how a candle can be 'stuck' into a candleholder by holding another lighted candle underneath it, so the base of the first candle melts.

Early Learning Goal
Show awareness of space, of themselves and others.

Talk About
Explain to the children that candles are put into a Hanukiah in a right-to-left direction, but lit in a left-to-right direction.

Further Ideas
- Play 'Marching Maccabees' games, using words such as 'left', 'right', 'quick march', 'about turn', 'halt' and so on.
- Turn an umbrella upside down and stick eight 'exercises' inside it. Let each child spin the umbrella driedel and move according to the spin.

Creative development

GLOWING CANDLES

What you need
Selection of metal or silver Hanukiot (if possible); one piece of white A4 paper for each child; 11 strips of aluminium foil (8cm by 3cm); pencils; glue; glue spreaders; wax crayons; thinly mixed blue powder paint; paintbrushes.

What to do
● Let the children examine the Hanukiot, if available. Invite them to notice the way that the metal or silver has been fashioned. Is it twisted or smooth? Does the Hanukiah have ridges in it?

● Encourage each child to make their own Hanukiah picture (see illustration). Invite them to use wax crayons to draw and colour in the candles and the candle flames, then paint a thin wash of blue paint over the candles, and around the outside of the Hanukiah.

Early learning Goal

Explore colour, texture, shape, form and space in two or three dimensions.

Talk About

Discuss the custom of standing a Hanukiah on a window ledge for people to see.

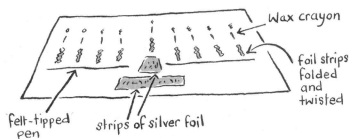

Wax crayon

foil strips folded and twisted

felt-tipped pen

strips of silver foil

TOOTHBRUSH PUPPETS

What you need
'Toothbrush puppets' photocopiable sheet on page 26; four new, inexpensive toothbrushes; 'The story of Hanukkah' photocopiable sheet on page 20; table; cardboard carton; three sheets of white A3 paper; felt-tipped pens; scissors; Blu-Tack.

What to do
● In groups of four, ask the children to colour in the puppets on the 'Toothbrush puppets' photocopiable sheet. Cut around the outline and slot each one into the bristles of a toothbrush, to make four puppets.
● Put the cardboard carton on its side on the table.
● Draw outline backgrounds representing King Antiochus' palace, a cave and the Jerusalem Temple (see illustration).
● Tell the children the story of Hanukkah.
● Narrate the story simply, as one pair of children at a time ('Antiochus', 'Judah' and then the two 'soldiers') push their puppets along the table and supply the dialogue.

Early learning Goal

Use their imagination in art and design, music, dance, imaginative and role play and stories.

Talk About

Say, for example, 'This is what King Antiochus shouted!' as the children tell the story.

Further Ideas

● Tell the key points of the story, asking everyone to make finger and hand movements, for example: Antiochus – finger wagging; Judah – finger pointing to caves and tapping his head to make him think; Maccabees – fingers 'marching' and hands 'scrubbing'; oil miracle – eight upright fingers; rejoicing – hand clapping.
● Draw around eight fingers, with one more in centre, to make a Hanukiah. Add glitter to make the Hanukiah sparkle.

CRAFT AND GIFT IDEAS

Creative development

HANUKKAH GELT BOXES

Early Learning Goal

Explore colour, texture, shape, form and space in two or three dimensions.

Group Size

Four children.

Support and Extension

With younger children, stick the card circles on the canisters beforehand. Instead of using and decorating double-sided tape, let older children wind parcel or metallic ribbon round their canisters, secured with sticky tape, or create weaving effects (see illustration).

Further Ideas

● Let the children make a container for loose change, as a Hanukkah gift, by covering a tall cylindrical crisp canister with plain coloured paper, and decorating it how they wish. Keep the transparent plastic lids to keep the coins safe.

● Make 'Hanukkah bags'. Explain that sometimes people give gifts of chocolate money in small bags. Encourage the children to wash their hands before wrapping up chocolate buttons, chocolate-covered raisins or sultanas in silver foil, and then put them in a 'bag' made from a paper-doily tied with ribbon. Add gift tags before giving the bags as a present.

What you need

For each child: one empty plastic 'wet wipes' canister (or similar shaped canister); piece of coloured A5 card; scissors; hole punch; piece of coloured A4 paper; sticky tape; coloured sticky tape; double-sided sticky tape; collage materials such as small pieces of crêpe paper; ribbon, metallic ribbon, sequins, buttons and so on; parcel ribbon; felt-tipped pens.

Preparation

Cut the A5 card in half. Cut one half into a circle the exact width of the canister, and cut a 'money slot' in the centre. Cut a rectangle (10cm by 5cm) from the other half of the card, and punch a hole at one end to make a gift tag.

What to do

● Explain that at Hanukkah, children are often given money called 'Hanukkah gelt'. They might receive one coin on the first night, two on the second, and so on. The whole family also gives money to charity.

● Invite the children to make Hanukkah gelt boxes, in which the whole family can put money to give to a charity.

● Help each child to stick a card circle on to the top of their canister, secured with sticky tape.

● Now invite the children to stick the coloured A4 paper around their canister.

● Show each child how to stick three bands of double-sided sticky tape around their canister, then let them decorate their canisters using the collage materials available.

● Decorate the spaces in between the bands using felt-tipped pens.

● Help each child, as necessary, to write 'Chag sameach' (Happy festival), the traditional Hanukkah greeting, on a gift tag.

● Thread parcel ribbon through the hole and attach the tag to the canister with sticky tape.

COOKERY IDEAS

Knowledge and understanding of the world

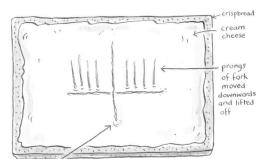

crispbread

cream cheese

prongs of fork moved downwards and lifted off

Lines made with toothpick

- After making and eating the latkes, recite the 'Lovely latkes' rhyme on page 22.
- Buy bags of pre-prepared frozen latkes from Jewish delicatessen stores, to cook in the oven.
- Have a Hanukkah snack time. Let each child spread cream cheese on a crispbread and use a fork and a toothpick to draw a Hanukiah in the cream cheese (see illustration above).
- Talk about the Turkish custom of having a special meal called a 'merenda' on the last night of Hanukkah, when everyone brings a contribution of food to share. Make a 'merenda' fruit salad. Ask the children to bring one piece of fruit to be cut up and added to a large mixing bowl with a little apple juice, to make a giant fruit salad.

LOVELY LATKES

What you need

Clean aprons; hand-washing facilities; six medium potatoes; potato peeler (adult use); 4 level tbsp self-raising flour; two eggs; salt; pepper; oil for frying; frying pan; spatula; kitchen roll; small bowl; fork; tablespoons; three large bowls; grater; three sieves; potato mashers; cooker.

Preparation

Just before the activity, peel and grate five potatoes, and put them in a large bowl. Check for any food allergies and dietary requirements.

What to do

1 Ask the children to wash their hands and put on clean aprons.
2 Explain that at Hanukkah, people enjoy eating foods cooked in oil, such as potato latkes and doughnuts. This reminds them about the miracle of the oil.
3 Let everyone watch you peel the remaining potato.
4 With very careful supervision, help each child have a turn at grating the potato into a large bowl, taking over yourself before the potato gets too small.
5 Add the grated potato to the bowl filled with the other potatoes, letting everyone stir with a tablespoon.
6 Divide the mixture between three sieves, resting over the large bowls, and leave to drain for about ten minutes. Explain that the water inside the potatoes will drain through the sieves, so that the latkes will taste crisp and not soggy. Meanwhile, let everyone take turns at beating the eggs with a fork in a small bowl.
7 Show the children the drained potato water. Explain that it is important to squeeze out as much water as possible, so that the hot oil won't 'spit'.
8 Let the group work in pairs to gently press on the grated potato with a masher.
9 Put all of the potato into one bowl and let everyone help to stir in the flour, seasoning and eggs.
10 An adult should fry tablespoons of the mixture in hot oil for about five minutes on each side.
11 Drain on kitchen paper until cool, and serve.

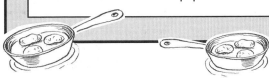

DISPLAY IDEAS

Mathematical development

GIANT HANUKIAH

What you need
The song 'The eight nights of Hanukkah' on page 22; display board; table; backing paper; corrugated paper border; staple gun; black felt-tipped pen; poster-sized sheet of white paper; eight white sticky labels; nine aerosol lids; nine cardboard tubes (from rolls of aluminium foil or similar); play brick; toilet tissue; nine A4-sized sheets of paper in various colours; scissors; sticky tape; one A5-sized piece of metallic paper or aluminium foil; household candle; matches (adult use).

Early Learning Goal
Find out one more or one less than a number from one to 10.

Group Size
Whole group.

What to do
● Follow the illustration to decorate the display board.
● Make nine 'candles' by covering each cardboard tube in different-coloured paper, and securing with sticky tape.
● Wrap the bottom of each tube in toilet tissue and put aside.
● Cut out nine 'flames' from the metallic paper or aluminium foil and put aside.
● Arrange the lids in a row on the table, with the central lid on top of the play brick.
● Stand one 'candle' – the shammash – inside the lid on the play brick.
● Write the numbers 1 to 8 on sticky labels and stick one on each lid, excluding the shammash, working from right to left.
● Each day, ask a child to place a 'candle' in a lid, starting on the right; one on the first day, two on the second and so on.
● Attach a 'flame' to the top of the shammash with sticky tape.
● Pretend to light a 'candle' daily by sticking a 'flame' on to each 'candle' with sticky tape. Make sure you 'light' them from left to right.
● Pretend to blow out the shammash flame each time, to save it.
● At the end of each day fold down the 'flames' ready for use the next day.
● Each day, sing an extra line from the song 'The eight nights of Hanukkah'.
● Light the real candle and hold it in your hand, to let everyone see the 'flickering flame dancing merrily'.
● As the children sing, invite them to hold up their fingers. Ask them to predict how many candles will be 'lit' tomorrow, and to show you using their fingers.
● Each day, point to the matching fact on the display board and talk about it.

Support and Extension
Ask younger children to show you how many candles are being lit that day. Ask older children to show you how many were lit yesterday.

Further Ideas
● Make a display of different kinds of Hanukiot made by the children using, for example, construction toys, junk items, play dough, clay and so on.
● Let the children experiment with making different kinds of driedels using milk cartons or circular cheese box lids, pierced by a pencil or other materials. Use them to make a display.

HANUKKAH
ROLE-PLAY IDEAS

Communication, language and literacy

PARTY TIME

What you need

Real Hanukiah with candles or a replica (see illustration); the rhyme 'Lovely latkes' on page 22; poster-sized sheet of white paper; felt-tipped pen; Blu-Tack; coloured A4 card; scissors; four balloons; one card driedel (see 'Driedel fun' activity on page 10); 40 counting cubes; five pieces of yellow sponge to represent latkes; toy oven; dolls.

Preparation

Cut the coloured A4 card into quarters. Draw a simple outline of a Hanukiah on the white sheet of paper and attach to a wall of the home corner with Blu-Tack. Cut out a 'shammash' candle from the coloured card and attach Blu-Tack to the back.

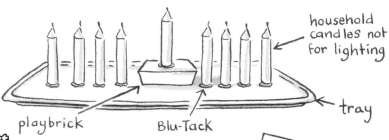

household candles not for lighting

tray

playbrick   Blu-Tack

'Shammash' candle cut from card with Blu-Tack on the back.

What to do

● Explain that you are going to have a pretend Hanukkah party in the home corner. Ask the children for ideas about what needs to be done, and in what order. For example, you might need to clean the home corner, make a shopping list of party food and decorations, buy the items, decorate the home corner and prepare the food.

● Let everyone join in the role-play, sticking balloons to the walls with Blu-Tack and making pretend latkes.

● When the 'latkes' are ready, ask one child to put them in a toy oven 'to keep them warm'.

● Recite all but the last verse of the 'Lovely latkes' action rhyme.

● When everything is ready, pretend to light the Hanukiah.

● Play some party games suggested by the children, then suggest playing a game where you pin the shammash on the Hanukiah. Let everyone in turn close their eyes and try to stick the 'shammash' in the right place in the central candleholder of the Hanukiah drawing.

● Invite the children to teach the dolls how to play the driedel game.

● Play a game of 'Hot and cold', giving clues such as 'very cold', 'getting warmer' and 'very hot' as one child tries to find a hidden 'latke' before it goes cold!

● After the party games join in with the children as they pretend to eat the party food. Bring the 'warm latkes' out of the toy oven as you all sing the last verse of 'Lovely latkes' and pretend to eat them.

Further Ideas

● Play a version of 'Goldilocks and the Three Bears', where Mummy Bear is preparing latkes for breakfast. End the story by having the Bears explain Hanukkah to Goldilocks, and inviting her to their Hanukiah lighting.

● Play 'Hanukkah gifts', giving each other one or more gifts on one of the nights of Hanukkah. For example, on the third night you would give three tiny gifts. Let the children wrap up items from around your setting, using sheets of used wrapping paper and a sticky-tape dispenser, or draw a picture of a gift, fold it, put it in a small box and wrap it up.

Personal, social and emotional development

Early Learning Goal

Have a developing respect for their own cultures and beliefs and those of other people.

Group Size

Whole group.

HAPPY HANUKKAH!

What you need

Hanukiah (real or home-made); nine Hanukkah candles or household candles with Blu-Tack on the base; matches (adult use); nine aluminium foil tubes covered in foil; one sheet of yellow A4 paper; scissors; eight sheets of white A4 paper; black felt-tipped pen; the song 'The eight nights of Hanukkah' on page 22; latkes (home-made) or eight small edible items representing 'Hanukkah gelt' for each child, such as chocolate buttons; low stool or box.

Preparation

Cut out nine 'flames' from the yellow paper and stick them on the top of the foil tubes, to make giant candles. Bend each flame downwards, so that the candle appears unlit. On each sheet of white paper, write a Hanukkah fact (see illustration of the display board on page 16). Before the celebration, give each sheet to eight children so that they can practise reading the words.

Nine household candles for lighting, secured inside lids with Blu-Tack

Aerosol lids, playbrick and tray all covered in silver foil.

What to do

● Ask eight children to stand in a row, each holding a giant candle and their fact sheet.
● Ask a ninth child to be the shammash and to stand on a low stool or box in the centre of the row, holding a giant candle, but not a fact sheet (see illustration below).

● Ask each child, in turn, moving in a right-to-left direction, to read out their fact sheet.
● As the fourth child speaks, ask the shammash child to raise their candle in the air.
● When the fifth child has spoken, let the shammash light each candle, moving in a left-to-right direction, with you lifting each flame upwards to make the candle appear lit.
● Light the Hanukiah and sing 'The eight nights of Hanukkah'.
● Encourage the children to wish each other 'Chag sameach' ('Happy festival').
● Serve the latkes or give everyone the edible Hanukkah gelt.

Support and Extension

Read the fact sheets yourself with younger children. After the fifth fact, help the shammash to light all the candles. Let individual older children show and talk about any model Hanukiot or driedels they have made.

Further Ideas

● Tell the Hanukkah story, accompanied by simple shadow puppets. Shine a light source behind a white screen and press and move card shapes up against the screen as you tell the story.
● Sit everyone in pairs, facing each other. One child, the 'Hanukiah', holds up eight fingers. Their partner, the shammash, touches the first child's fingers in turn (left to right) while everyone recites: One, two, three, four, five, six, seven, eight!
Hanukkah's here – let's celebrate! Chag sameach!

DANCE IDEAS

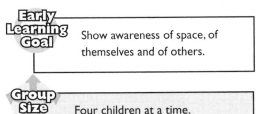

DRIEDEL DANCE

Early Learning Goal
Show awareness of space, of themselves and of others.

Group Size
Four children at a time.

What you need
Copy of the 'Driedel song' on page 22; one umbrella; four sheets of white A5 paper; scissors; black felt-tipped pen; 16 small counting cubes in four colours (four cubes in each colour); tray; large floor space.

Preparation
Using the illustration as a reference, draw four instructions on the four pieces of A5 paper. Stick these on to alternate sections of an upturned umbrella. Put the umbrella in the centre of the floor space. Put the cubes in colour sets on the tray next to the umbrella.

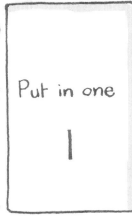

Take Nothing O | Take all | Take half | Put in one 1

Support and Extension
Ask younger children to twirl and make the appropriate movements on the spot, without moving or dancing across the floor. With older children, add the final verse from the song, helping the children by pointing your arm left and right.

Further Ideas
● Match the sound of a percussion instrument to how the driedels should move, for example: fast – tambourine; slow – drum; high – triangle; low – guiro. Instead of singing the song, play an instrument for the driedel to move to, accordingly.

What to do
● Ask the children to join in with the words to the 'Driedel song' on page 22, and invite everyone to be a dancing driedel as you sing.
● Invite four children to stand around the umbrella, and explain that it is a giant driedel.
● Let the children choose a colour and put one cube in a 'kitty' on the tray.
● Give each child their remaining three cubes, asking them to make two fists, with two cubes in one hand and one cube in the other hand.
● Remove the umbrella and the tray, and ask each child to stand in a space of their own with arms outstretched, still holding the cubes.
● Encourage them to twirl around and to move in and out between one another, as if they were driedels dancing across the floor.
● Sing the 'Driedel song' again, encouraging the children to twirl 'quickly', 'slowly', 'high' and 'low'.
● When everyone has stopped twirling, put the umbrella and tray back in the centre of the floor space.
● Ask each child, in turn, to spin the giant driedel and to follow the instruction with their cubes.
● When each child has had a turn, encourage them to count how many cubes they have.

THE STORY OF HANUKKAH

Long, long ago there was a fierce and unkind king called Antiochus. He told the Jewish people that they were not allowed to live how they wanted to any more. He said that they had to do everything he said and that they were not allowed to pray to God and study the Jewish Bible, called the Torah. King Antiochus and his soldiers marched into the beautiful temple in Jerusalem where the Jewish people prayed to God. Antiochus and his soldiers made the Jewish people leave the temple. The Jewish people were very, very sad.

Then an old and wise Jewish priest called Mattathias said, 'We must not be afraid! Let's pray to God to help us fight against King Antiochus and his soldiers!'. Mattathias had five sons. The bravest was called Judah Maccabee. Judah said, 'Let's go and live in the caves and think what to do about King Antiochus'. The people who heard him said, 'Yes, we will live in the caves with you', and they called themselves the Maccabees.

It was cold and dark in the caves and there wasn't much food, but the Maccabees were brave and strong. They made careful plans and, after a long time, Judah and the Maccabees won against King Antiochus and his soldiers, although the king had many, many more soldiers than Judah. The Maccabees made Antiochus and his soldiers leave the temple.

When the Maccabees went inside the temple they were very shocked and sad. Everything was broken and dirty, and in a terrible mess. They worked very hard indeed at cleaning, scrubbing, sweeping, dusting and mending everything. They wanted to light the gold temple lamp, called the Menorah, but one of the Maccabees could only find a tiny amount of pure olive oil, just enough to last for one day. He put the oil in the Menorah and lit it. Eight days later his friend said, 'Look! The oil is still burning!'. By that time new oil had been made.

To this day, at Hanukkah time, Jewish families light candles every night for eight nights, in a special Hanukkah Menorah called a Hanukiah, to say thank you to God for helping the Maccabees win against King Antiochus, and for making the oil last for eight days.

Linda Mort

Eight special gifts

One – a sunny smile, oh so wide
Makes friends feel happy – inside!

Two – a gentle hug, like a bear
Shows everyone that we care.

Three – if we blow a friendly kiss
Everyone will smile at this!

Four – let's make someone laugh – it's
fun to do
For everyone, and me and you!

Five – let's do a job to help someone
And we will have a lot of fun!

Six – let's share with someone what we eat
And they'll say 'thank you' for the treat!

Seven – there are lots of games that
we can play
With lots of people every day.

Eight – let's share a book, side by side
And we will smile – very wide!

All these things, as we can see
Can make us happy as can be!

Linda Mort

What shall we use?

(Sung to the tune of 'What shall we do
with the Drunken Sailor?')

What shall we use to clean our carpets?
(Repeat twice.)
Because they're looking dirty!

Let's all push our vacuum cleaners.
(Repeat twice.)
Forwards and backwards!

What shall we use to clean our baths?
(Repeat twice.)
Because there are some tide marks!

Let's all use our squeezy sponges.
(Repeat twice.)
To rub away the tide marks!

What shall we do to clean the cobwebs?
(Repeat twice.)
They're in lots of corners!

Let's all use our feather dusters.
(Repeat twice.)
To dust away the cobwebs!

Linda Mort

HANUKKAH RHYMES

Lovely latkes

Peel the potato, (Repeat twice.)
With great care!

Grate the potato, (Repeat twice.)
With great care!

Beat the egg, (Repeat twice.)
With great care!

Mix in the flour,
And the salt and pepper,
Mix in the egg
With great care!

Fry all the latkes, (Repeat twice.)
With great care!

The latkes are ready, (Repeat twice.)
Let's all share!

Linda Mort

The eight nights of Hanukkah

(Sung to the tune of 'The Twelve Days of Christmas')

(Hold up the relevant number of fingers for each verse and wiggle them to represent flickering flames)

On the first night of Hanukkah
What do we see?
One flickering flame
Dancing merrily!

On the second night of Hanukkah
What do we see?
Two flickering flames
Dancing merrily!

(And so on, up to eight)

Linda Mort

Driedel song

(Sung to the tune of 'Twinkle, Twinkle, Little Star')

Driedels spinning round and round
Quickly, quickly, without a sound!

Driedels spinning round and round
Slowly, slowly, to the ground.

Driedels spinning high and low
This is the way that driedels go!

(For older children, add...)
Driedels spin to the left and right
Driedels are a pretty sight!

Linda Mort

Invitation to

Please come to the Hanukkah party

Love from

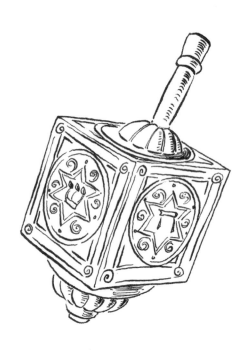

Hebrew letter	Name of letter	Meaning in game
נ	nun	nothing (player receives nothing)
ג	gimmel	all (player gets all the 'kitty')
ה	hay	half (player gets half of 'kitty')
ש	shin	put (share) (player puts in one)

Instructions for making a card driedel

Cut out and stick on to card. Make a hole in the centre with an awl and push
a matchstick through the hole to make a spinner.

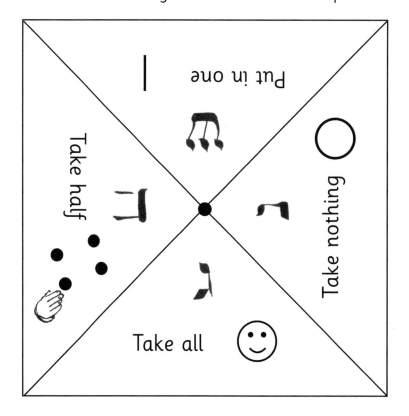

Match the pictures to the words with a line.

Torah scroll

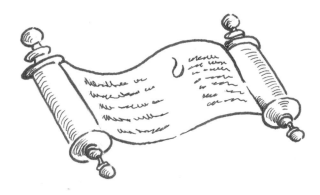

Star of David

Kippah

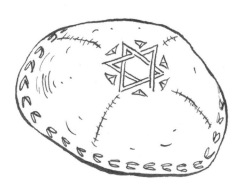

Synagogue

TOOTHBRUSH PUPPETS

King Antiochus	Judah Maccabee

First Maccabee who noticed there was only one drop of oil left in the temple lamp.	Second Maccabee who realised the oil had lasted for eight days!

BACKGROUND INFORMATION AND PLANNING

Dates

● Rosh Hashana, the Jewish New Year, always occurs in September or October. Orthodox Jewish people celebrate the festival over a two-day period, and Reform Jews celebrate for one day.

● Rosh Hashana falls on the following dates over the next three years:

16 September 2004 (Jewish year 5765)
04 October 2005 (Jewish year 5766)
23 September 2006 (Jewish year 5767)

The festival begins at sunset on the day before the dates shown above. Dates beyond 2006 can be found on the website: www.jewishpeople.net/jewishholidays.html

Religious beliefs

Rosh Hashana is the Hebrew for 'head of the year' ('rosh' meaning 'head', and 'shana' meaning 'year'). The festival occurs at the beginning of a ten-day period of self-examination and reflection, known as the 'Days of Penitence', which end with the Fast day of Yom Kippur – the 'Day of Atonement'. Children, elderly and sick people are not required to fast. Rosh Hashana is known by several different names, each with its own significance. The 'New Year' is the most well-known name. Rosh Hashana occurs in autumn, because this is seen as the end of the year's natural cycle, when the harvests are gathered and there is a short time of rest before the year's tasks are started again. The festival is also known as the 'birthday of the world', as it is believed that God created the universe at this time.

Other names for the festival are the 'Day of Judgement' and the 'Day of Memorial', when it is believed that God judges and remembers everyone in relation to their behaviour during the previous year.

Rosh Hashana is also known as the 'Day of sounding the shofar' (ram's horn). The shofar is blown in the synagogue as a spiritual wake-up call to everyone to remember God and to think about their behaviour, both good and bad, during the previous year, and how it can be improved for everyone's benefit by making 'New Year resolutions' to be a better person.

Customs and traditions

It is customary to greet people by saying 'Shana tova', which means 'a good year' ('shana' means 'year' and 'tova' means 'good'). This is a shortened version of 'Leshana tova tikatavu', which means 'may you be inscribed for a good new year' because, according to tradition, at Rosh Hashana the sounds of the shofar reach God's ears and remind Him to open the Book of Life and immediately write down the names of good people so that they will be happy during the year to come.

People who have not behaved well will be judged again by God on Yom Kippur, so giving them time

Happy New Year

שנה טובה

to repent and change during the Days of Penitence between Rosh Hashana and Yom Kippur. (The Hebrew for 'Days of Penitence' literally means 'Days of return'.) Jewish people send New Year cards to each other, on which they write one of the greetings.

It is the custom at Rosh Hashana to wear new clothes, to give gifts of plants and to eat foods sweetened with honey and dried fruits, to symbolise a good and sweet year.

Celebrations

Families celebrate Rosh Hashana in the home by eating symbolic food. On the first night of the festival, blessings are recited over candles, wine is sipped and special holiday challah bread is eaten. The bread is baked in a round shape, instead of the usual plaited loaf. This is to signify the cyclical nature of life. At the festival, the challah can be baked with raisins for extra sweetness. The challah is dipped in honey and then more blessings are recited before and after everyone dips an apple slice in honey, for a good and sweet year. More apple and honey are eaten the next day, after families return from the synagogue.

On the second day of the festival, people eat a new seasonal fruit, such as a pomegranate or pineapple, also with a special blessing.

Things to remember

Jewish people believe in one God who created the universe. Jews believe that God revealed the Torah to Moses on Mount Sinai. 'Torah' means 'the law' or 'instruction', and teaches Jews how to live in order to be good people, as well as how the world was created and the early history of the Jewish people. The Torah is read in sections in the synagogue every week. It takes a year to read the Torah. Another name for the Torah is the 'Five books of Moses' (the Old Testament). The Torah includes the Ten Commandments. In addition to 'Torah' meaning the 'Five books of Moses', the word is usually used to include the further books of the Jewish Bible and the whole body of Jewish teaching, from biblical times until now. Jewish people carry out God's wishes by following the laws of the Torah in practice. At Rosh Hashana, Jews believe that it is not sufficient for a person to apologise to God in prayer for wrong behaviour. Anyone who has been wronged must be apologised to in person, and amends made.

The Torah is written by hand in Hebrew on parchment scrolls covered in cloth decorated with silver.

Using the poster

Display the poster and explain to the children that the challah loaf has been baked in a round shape specially for Rosh Hashana, to remind everyone that a new year has 'come round again'. Write the months of the year round the edge of a large piece of circular paper. Chant the months together, showing how each child grows older by one year. Explain also that the round shape reminds people of the round crown of God. Point to the raisins and sultanas in the bread and tell the children that these, as well as honey, have been added to the challah dough for 'a sweet year'.

ROSH HASHANA
FESTIVAL PLANNER

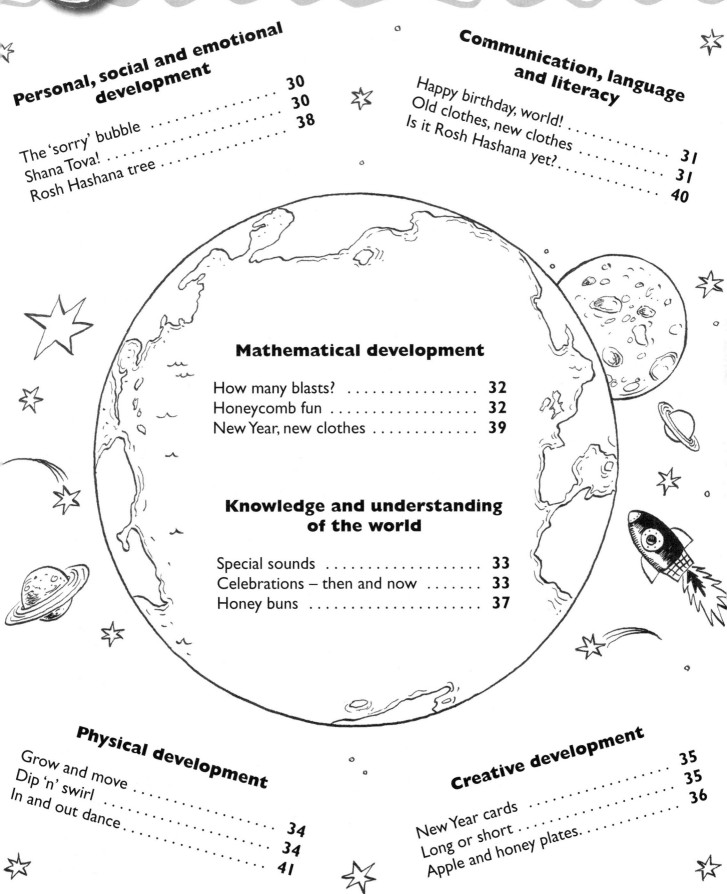

CROSS-CURRICULAR IDEAS

Personal, social and emotional development

Have a developing awareness of their own needs, views and feelings and be sensitive to the needs, views and feelings of others.

Talk About Tell the children that, at Rosh Hashana, people make New Year resolutions to be kind to everyone during the next year.

Early Learning Goal Understand that people have different needs, views, cultures and beliefs, that need to be treated with respect.

Talk About Tell the children that in Hebrew, 'Shana' means 'year' and 'tova' means 'good'.

Further Ideas
● Explain that at Rosh Hashana, people eat pomegranates in the hope that they will be able to do as many kind things as there are seeds in the pomegranate. Invite the children to count the pips in an apple and plan a good deed for each one.
● Let pairs of children use glove puppets to demonstrate gentle disagreements, ending with apologies.
● Draw a large picture of the inside of a beehive, showing how all the bees have special jobs and work together.

THE 'SORRY' BUBBLE

What you need
Sheet of A3 card; felt-tipped pen; scissors.

What to do
● Draw a speech bubble on the A3 card and write the word 'Sorry' inside. Cut out the speech bubble.
● Sit in a circle and explain that at Rosh Hashana, people think about whether they have been kind during the last year, and whether they said sorry for making anybody sad.
● Hold up the 'Sorry' bubble and talk about when someone apologised to you, or when you apologised. If necessary, make up an example, such as accidentally bumping into someone and saying sorry.
● Pass the 'Sorry' bubble around, asking everyone to talk about when someone said sorry to them, or when they said sorry.

SHANA TOVA!

What you need
The song 'Shana Tova' on page 43; a child's glove; aluminium foil tube.

What to do
● Put the glove on the end of the tube.
● Sing the song, letting everyone shake hands using the tube.

Communication, language and literacy

HAPPY BIRTHDAY, WORLD!

Early Learning Goal
Listen with enjoyment, and respond to stories, songs and other music, rhymes and poems, and make up their own stories, songs, rhymes and poems.

Talk About
Explain that many Jewish people believe that the age of the world (for example at Rosh Hashana 2004) to be 5765 years (see 'Background information and planning' on page 27).

What you need
The song 'Happy birthday world!' on page 44; globe; pictures or illustrations of the items mentioned in the song, for example, sun, moon and stars.

What to do
● Hold up the globe and talk about it with the children.
● Tell the children that people say that Rosh Hashana is the world's birthday.
● Sing the song together, holding up the relevant pictures.
● Ask everyone to think of three more words from different categories for each verse, for example weather, animals or food.

OLD CLOTHES, NEW CLOTHES

Early Learning Goal
Speak clearly and audibly with confidence and control and show awareness of the listener, for example by their use of conventions such as greetings, 'please' and 'thank you'.

Talk About
Talk about the Rosh Hashana tradition of wearing new clothes to attend synagogue.

What you need
Items of children's clothing, for example, coat, t-shirt, trousers, dress, shoes, pyjamas and nightdress.

What to do
● Sit the children in a circle around the clothes on the floor, and explain how people like to wear new clothes at Rosh Hashana.
● Talk about old clothes and new clothes. Invite the children to discuss when they receive and wear new clothes, for example, at a birthday party or when they have grown out of their old clothes.
● Ask each child to choose an item from the clothes in the centre of the circle, without touching it, and say, 'I used to have an old…, which was… (colour, design and so on) but my new one is… (description)'.

Further Ideas
● Explain to the children how apple slices are dipped in honey at Rosh Hashana for a good, sweet year. Do they know where honey comes from? Use seed catalogues to find the names of flowers, and enjoy reciting the rhyme:
Mary, Mary, quite contrary
How does your garden grow?
With lots of trees and honey bees
And (for example) dahlias all in a row.

CROSS-CURRICULAR IDEAS

Mathematical development

HOW MANY BLASTS?

What you need
Sticky tape; seven pieces of A4 paper.

What to do
● Roll the paper up to make seven shofarot (plural of shofar).
● Blow a 'shofar', making a few vocalised blasts at intervals and ask everyone to count. Assign a number up to five to each child in a group of five children.

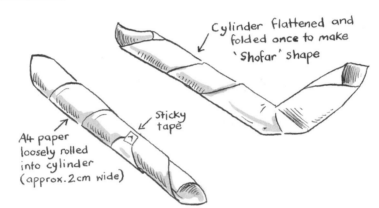

Cylinder flattened and folded once to make 'Shofar' shape

Sticky tape

A4 paper loosely rolled into cylinder (approx. 2cm wide)

● Give a 'shofar' to a sixth child and ask them to sound any number of blasts up to five for everyone to count.
● Invite the child who was assigned that number in the group to become the new shofar blower.

HONEYCOMB FUN

What you need
Piece of honeycomb (you can find this inside jars of comb honey, available from larger supermarkets); magnifying glasses; 'Honeycomb hexagon' photocopiable sheet on page 45; scissors.

Preparation
Make one copy of the 'Honeycomb hexagon' photocopiable sheet for each child and cut out the hexagon shapes.

What to do
● Invite everyone to examine the piece of honeycomb with magnifying glasses. Notice how the hexagon shapes fit together. Tell the children that the shapes tessellate.
● Say the rhyme together and do the accompanying finger actions. Now encourage the children to work together to fit their hexagons together on the floor. Can they make a giant honeycomb?

Knowledge and understanding of the world

Early Learning Goal Find out about, and identify, the uses of everyday technology and use information and communication technology and programmable toys to support their learning.

Talk About Tell the children that a shofar (ram's horn) is blown in synagogues on Rosh Hashana as a signal to remind people to think about being kind.

Early Learning Goal Find out about past and present events in their own lives, and in those of their families and other people they know.

Talk About Try a game of 'apple spinning', played in Edwardian England at Rosh Hashana. Two children each spin a small apple on a tray. The child whose apple spins the longest wins.

Further Ideas
● Demonstrate the use of a peeler, corer and grater in preparing apples. Stress that the children must never use these.
● Explain that dried fruits are popular at Rosh Hashana. Match the fresh and dried versions of apples, apricots and bananas, plums and grapes.
● Make a fruit compote.

SPECIAL SOUNDS

What you need
'Can you hear?' photocopiable sheet on page 46; scissors; shoebox.

What to do
● Cut out the pictures on the photocopiable sheet and put them in the shoebox.
● Ask eight children to each pick a picture from the box.
● Invite each child with a 'special sound' picture to make the sound and say how it is made (such as whether an electronic computer chip is used, or not).
● Encourage the children to put themselves into pairs by matching up the sound pictures with the action pictures.

CELEBRATIONS – THEN AND NOW

What you need
Computer and printer; A3 sheets of white paper; sugar paper; felt-tipped pens; hole punch; ribbon.

What to do
● Type up and print out a letter (see illustration below) to send home to parents.
● When you get the information back, type up the details. Enlarge them and print them on to A3 paper, then make the details into a book. Let the children illustrate it.
● Chat about how celebrations are the same today, and how they have changed.

Dear Families,
    We are learning about how people celebrate the Festival of Rosh Hashana, the Jewish New Year.
    Could you please jot down a few sentences about any family religious or traditional celebrations, either from the past or now, for our special book called 'Celebrations – then and now'.
    Thank you very much,
                from

CROSS-CURRICULAR IDEAS

Physical development

GROW AND MOVE

Move with control and co-ordination.

Hold up the Rosh Hashana card. Say that the card is like a birthday card for the world and that each year the world gets older. Explain that the world was young a very long time ago, and that there were no buildings, cars or aeroplanes then.

What you need
Home-made Rosh Hashana card (see illustration); one birth congratulations card; children's birthday cards aged one to five (one of each); the rhyme 'Grow and move' on page 43.

What to do
● Hold up each card in turn and talk about the different things that babies, toddlers and children learn to do.
● Say the rhyme on the sheet together.
● Recite the rhyme again, this time holding up the cards. Encourage the children to demonstrate the movements in the rhyme.

DIP 'N' SWIRL

Handle tools, objects, construction and malleable materials safely and with increasing control.

Tell the children that at Rosh Hashana, people like to eat sweet treats that they have made themselves.

What you need
One stoned date or dried, washed apricot for each child; clear honey; desiccated coconut; small pair of tongs (such as sugar tongs) or teabag squeezer; plate; aluminium foil; hand-washing facilities.

What to do
● Explain to the children how people enjoy eating new fruits and sweet treats, such as honey, at Rosh Hashana.
● Check for any food allergies and dietary requirements.
● Cover the plate in foil.
● Ask everyone to wash their hands.
● Invite each child to pick up the date or apricot with the tongs and to dip it in the honey and then in the coconut. Encourage them to place their date or apricot on the plate.
● Refrigerate for 30 minutes then enjoy at snack time!

● Play a paper shofar (see 'How many blasts?' activity on page 32), a recorder, a whistle and other wind instruments. Let everyone agree on a different movement or shape for each sound.
● Invite the children to pretend to be bees working in a hive, and make up movements for looking after the baby bees, cleaning and keeping the hive cool.
● Ask the children to use a fishing net to fish for apples that are bobbing in water.

Creative development

NEW YEAR CARDS

What you need

For each child: 'Make a card' photocopiable sheet on page 47; A4 card; glue; awl (adult use); piece of wool (10cm long); sticky tape; felt-tipped pens.

What to do

● Fold each piece of card widthways and make a hole with an awl in the front, top, right-hand corner (see illustration).
● Ask each child to colour in the bee and write their name underneath 'Love from'. Help them, as necessary, to cut out the rectangles.
● When they have finished making the card, encourage the children to decorate the front and inside with felt-tipped pens.

Early Learning Goal

Explore colour, texture, shape, form and space in two or three dimensions.

Talk About

Explain that some Rosh Hashana cards bought in shops open from right to left, like the Siddur (Jewish prayer book).

flowers drawn by child in felt-tipped pen

Shana Tova Happy New Year

Greeting cut out and stuck on card

10 cm of wool attached with adhesive tape and threaded through hole

Cut-out bee

End of wool secured with adhesive tape

love from Sarah XX

Message cut out and stuck on card

LONG OR SHORT

Early Learning Goal

Recognise and explore how sounds can be changed, sing simple songs from memory, recognise repeated sounds and sound patterns and match movements to music.

Talk About

Explain that, at Rosh Hashana, the person blowing the shofar in synagogue must blow it in special patterns, using very long, long, short, and very short blasts.

What you need

Paper 'shofar' for each child (see 'How many blasts?' activity on page 32); six thick straws in one bright shade (for example, pink or green); scissors; sticky tape.

What to do

● Cut and join the straws end-to-end with sticky tape, to make one very long straw, one long straw, one short and one very short straw (see illustration).

One and a half straws, to denote a 'long' blast

● Hold up each straw horizontally and ask the children to blow short or long blasts with their 'shofars' (shofarot) depending on the length of the straw.

Further Ideas

● Let the children use pencil crayons to recreate the different shading on various kinds of apples.
● Invite each child to draw a bee on card. Cut them out and attach them to string to hover over real or artificial flowers.

Creative development

APPLE AND HONEY PLATES

What you need

Large white paper plates; small doilies (gold, if possible); small plastic plate or mousse pots; glue; glue spreaders; scissors; hole punch; variety of decorative materials such as tissue and crêpe paper, coloured paper, glitter, feathers, sequins, buttons, parcel and fabric ribbon, brightly coloured thick wool and metallic twine; white A4 paper; pen.

What to do

● On one sheet of A4 paper, write the following: 'It is Rosh Hashana, the Jewish New Year. _____ (child's name) has made this apple and honey plate. Please fill the dish with honey, and put slices of apple around the dish. Everyone dips their apple in the honey, and says "Shana Tova"! (Have a good and sweet year!) to everyone else.'
● Draw a picture of the plate at the bottom of the sheet. Make one copy of the sheet for each child.

● Give the children one large plate each and invite them to decorate the rim of their plate as they wish, for example, by gluing on buttons, sequins and so on, and small pieces of coloured paper cut into different shapes. Alternatively, each child could punch holes around the rim and thread ribbon, wool or twine through the holes.
● When each child's plate is decorated, invite everyone to glue a small doily in the centre of the plate.
● Encourage each child to glue a small plastic pot in the centre of their doily.
● Let everyone take home their apple and honey plate with a copy of the sheet.

Knowledge and understanding of the world

Early Learning Goal

Look closely at similarities, differences, patterns and change.

Group Size

Six children.

Support and Extension

Let younger children watch you beating the egg. Older children could write the letter 'h' (for honey) on each cooled bun, using a small tube of writing icing.

Further Ideas

● Demonstrate the use of an apple corer to core a dessert apple for each child. Let the children place sultanas and a little honey inside the apples. Score around the centre of each apple and bake in a greased ovenproof dish with a little water for one hour, at Gas Mark 5 (375°F/190°C).

● Invite the children to taste a small cube of pineapple together with a small cube of mild cheese. Talk about sweet and savoury tastes.

● Let everyone make a sandwich with brown bread, margarine, honey and apple rings.

HONEY BUNS

What you need

Ingredients (makes two buns per child): small egg; 60g soft margarine; 60g soft brown sugar; 3 tbsp runny honey; ¼ tsp bicarbonate of soda; 60ml warm water (boiled); 110g plain flour; level tsp powdered ginger; pinch of mixed sweet spice.

Equipment: hand-washing facilities; aprons; small plastic bowl; small fork; weighing scales; tablespoon; dessert spoon; teaspoon; measuring jug; bun tin; paper baking cases; two large mixing bowls; wooden spoon; sieve; small plastic plate; wire cooling tray.

Preparation

Set the oven to Gas Mark 5 (375°F/190°C). Dissolve the bicarbonate of soda in the water in the measuring jug. Check for any food allergies and dietary requirements.

What to do

● Ask the children to wash their hands and to put on an apron.

● Crack the egg into the small plastic bowl.

● Let everyone practise a beating motion, by making a fist and flicking their wrist.

● Pass the fork around, and let everyone take turns at beating the egg.

● Weigh the margarine and sugar and put in a large mixing bowl.

● Let everyone have a go at mixing it with the wooden spoon.

● Add the egg and let everyone take turns at mixing.

● Add the honey and take turns to mix it in.

● Weigh the flour and leave it on the scales.

● Take turns to sieve the flour, ginger and spice into a large mixing bowl.

● Pour the flour, ginger and spice alternately with the dissolved bicarbonate of soda into the creamed honey and sugar mixture.

● Stir the mixture into a thin batter.

● Help each child, as necessary, to put two dessert spoons of batter into two paper baking cases on a small plate, and then into the bun tin.

● Bake in the middle of the oven for 20–25 minutes, until golden brown and spongy to the touch.

● Cool on a wire tray. Enjoy your treats at snack time.

Personal, social and emotional development

ROSH HASHANA TREE

What you need

Display board; pale blue frieze paper (1.2m by 1m); staple gun (adult use); glue; glue spreaders; brown, green and red paint; mixing palettes; saucers; small sponges; paintbrushes; painting aprons; red wavy border; three sheets of white A4 paper; child scissors; two sheets of red A4 card; two sheets of yellow A4 card; sticky tape; 32cm string; pencil; black felt-tipped pens; four small plastic tea-towel hooks.

Preparation

Fold the sheets of red and yellow A4 card and two sheets of A4 paper into quarters and cut them out. Fill the palettes with brown and red paint. Put green paint in the saucers.

What to do

- Ask six children to put on aprons.
- In pencil, draw a simple outline of a leafless tree on the frieze paper.
- Ask the children to fill in the outline with brown paint.
- When dry, encourage the children to sponge-paint green leaves on to the tree outline.
- Next, give each child one of the quarter-sized pieces of A4 paper and ask them to paint a red apple on to their piece.

- Let the children cut out their apples and glue them on to the frieze paper.
- Staple the frieze paper and border on to a display board.
- Cut a sheet of white A4 paper in half, vertically, and write the heading 'Our Rosh Hashana tree' on it. Stick it above the tree outline.
- Stick the four plastic hooks randomly on to the tree.
- Meanwhile, ask four children to draw a large apple shape on quarter-sized pieces of red and yellow card and to cut them out.
- Help each child to join their red and yellow shapes together, side-by-side, with sticky tape, to make an apple book.
- Help to write, copy or overwrite the wording (or similar) in the illustrations, using a black felt-tipped pen on the red, left-hand side of the apple book.

- Ask each child to draw a picture on the yellow, right-hand side.
- Attach a piece of string to each apple book and hang them on the tree.

Mathematical development

NEW YEAR, NEW CLOTHES

What you need

Five chairs; small fleece; each child's own fleece or jacket; sheet of white A5 paper; two sheets of A4 coloured paper; pen; scissors; sticky tape; Blu-Tack; wooden ruler; shoebox lid; sheet of A4 white paper.

Preparation

Cut the white A5 paper into four strips, each 7cm by 2cm. Write, for example, 'Age 3–4' and 'Age 4–5' on the strips, as appropriate, and stick them inside the collars of the children's fleeces or jackets with sticky tape. Use discretion in the case of very small or very tall children. Make four paper 'toecaps' (see illustration, right), by drawing four semi-circles, each 4cm wide and 3cm deep, on each piece of coloured A4 paper. Cut them out. Make a shoe-size measure (see illustration, left). Set up the home corner as a clothes and shoe shop. Cut a strip 2cm wide from the side of the white A4 paper and mark it in centimetres.

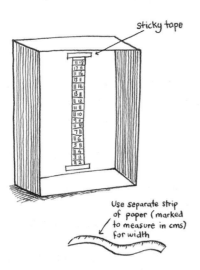

sticky tape

Use separate strip of paper (marked to measure in cms) for width

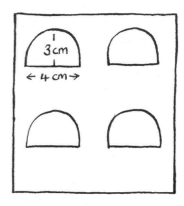

3cm

← 4 cm →

What to do

● Explain that at Rosh Hashana, the Jewish New Year, people like to buy new clothes to wear in synagogue and when visiting their family and friends.

● Say that everyone in the group has grown during the past year, and that they are too big to wear the smallest fleece.

● Let them try it on, saying if it is too big, too small or just right.

● Invite the children to sit on the chairs and explain that you will pretend to be a shop assistant.

● Ask everyone to say how old they are.

● Offer each child their own fleece or jacket to try on, pointing out the age label.

● Stick each pair of paper semi-circular toecaps on the front of each child's shoes with Blu-Tack. Explain that this is so you can pretend that the shoes are old and too small.

● Help one child to remove his or her shoes. Note the size, but do not mention it to the group.

● Measure the child's feet with the shoe-size measure and say, 'You need to wear size…'.

● Remove the 'toecaps' from the child's shoes and hold up the shoes.

● Say, for example, 'Here is a new pair of shoes in your size, which is size…'.

● Repeat with the rest of the group.

● Let everyone pretend to pay you for their purchases.

Communication, language and literacy

IS IT ROSH HASHANA YET?

Early Learning Goal

Listen with enjoyment and respond to stories, songs and other music, rhymes and poems and make up their own stories, songs, rhymes and poems.

Group Size

Whole group.

Support and Extension

Remind younger children that Rosh Hashana is always in the season of autumn. Recite the chant, 'spring blossom – summer sun – autumn leaves – winter snow' several times, with everyone clapping their hands. Ask older children whether they know of any other festivals. Can they tell you the seasons in which they occur?

Further Ideas

● Make a 'Festivals and their seasons' wall chart.
● Before serving apple slices and honey, let the children dip a small piece of pitta bread in hummus mixed with pomegranate kernels.
● Play a game of 'Happy world'. Stick a paper smiley face on to an inflatable globe with sticky tape. Sit everyone in a circle and pass the globe around to music. When the music stops, whoever is holding the globe should say, 'It makes the whole world happy when people…', using their own suggestions.

What you need

The story 'Is it Rosh Hashana yet?' on page 42; the song 'Is it Rosh Hashana?' on page 44; Rosh Hashana tree display (optional – see 'Rosh Hashana tree' activity on page 38); one or more Jewish New Year cards (home-made or bought); jar of honey; small dish; apple slices; lemon juice; plate.

Preparation

Display the Rosh Hashana tree (if used) where everyone can see it. Put the honey in the dish, arrange the apple slices on the plate and sprinkle with lemon juice.

What to do

● Hold up the Jewish New Year cards and say that it is Rosh Hashana.
● Help four children, as necessary, to read the four apple books on the Rosh Hashana tree (if used). If you are not using the display, explain that at Rosh Hashana, Jewish people go to synagogue to hear the shofar (ram's horn), and to wish one another 'Shana Tova' (Happy New Year). Remind the children that people eat apple and honey and pomegranates or pineapple.
● Ask everyone to stand in a space of their own and to join in with the action song 'Is it Rosh Hashana?'.
● Let everyone dip an apple slice in the honey, and wish each other 'Shana Tova!'.

Physical development

Early Learning Goal

Show awareness of space, of themselves and of others.

Group Size

18 children.

IN AND OUT DANCE

What you need
Large floor space; six plastic flowers; three sheets of red A4 paper; scissors.

Preparation
Fold each sheet of red paper into quarters and cut out an apple shape, making 12 shapes in total.

What to do
● Ask six children to stand in a circle with their arms outstretched. Explain that they are the apple trees.
● Give each child a paper apple shape to hold in each hand.
● Place the plastic flowers in the centre of the circle.
● Ask six more children to be flying bees, skipping in the same direction in and out of the trees.
● Explain that each bee is looking for a flower, so that it can lap up nectar and fly away to the beehive where the nectar will be made into honey.
● Encourage everyone to sing the following rhyme, to the tune of 'In and Out the Bonny Bluebells', as the bees fly around:
    In and out the apple trees (*Repeat twice more*)
    The bees are looking for flowers.
● Ask the bees to pretend to lap up nectar from one flower each, as everyone sings:
    Buzz, buzz, buzz – they have found some (*Repeat twice more*)
    What a lot of nectar!
● Ask the bees to fly back to the hive and rejoin the rest of the group. Invite everyone to sing:
    Now the bees fly back to the hive (*Repeat twice more*)
    To make some yummy honey!
● Invite six different children to be farmers, walking in and out between the trees, as you sing together:
    Now the farmers take a walk (*Repeat twice more*)
    Looking for some apples.
● Ask each farmer to pick two apples from one tree, as the whole group sings:
    Now the farmers pick the apples (*Repeat twice more*)
    They're all ready to eat!
● Finish the dance by asking everyone to pretend to dip apple into honey and eat it, as they sing:
    Now we have our apple and honey (*Repeat twice more*)
    Because it's Rosh Hashana!

Support and Extension

With younger children, reduce the number to 12, and have four children in each set. With older children, ask half the bees and half the farmers to move in opposite directions.

Further Ideas

● Explain that when bees go out looking for nectar, they visit only one kind of flower during that outing. Increase the number of flowers to 18, using six different colours, with three flowers in each colour. Use flower-shaped construction pieces if necessary. Ask each bee to visit three of the same kind of flower as everyone sings the second verse of the song.
● Cut out extra red paper apples and stick them on the front and back of the 'trees' with sticky tape. Ask each farmer to pick a certain number of apples, as everyone sings the fifth verse of the song.

For such a long time, Amy and Ben, the twins, had been watching their apple tree in the garden. In the springtime, the tree was covered in white blossom.

'Is it Rosh Hashana yet?' asked the twins.

'No, not yet,' said the grown-ups. In the summer, the tree was covered in green leaves and very, very tiny baby apples.

'Is it Rosh Hashana yet?' asked the twins.

'No, not yet,' said the grown-ups. Today, the tree was covered in big apples, and the garden was covered in brown leaves.

'Is it Rosh Hashana yet?' asked the twins.

'Yes', said Mum, Dad and Grandpa David, who had come to stay. 'It is autumn now, and Rosh Hashana starts tonight!'

All day, the twins helped to clean and tidy the house. They tidied their room properly and helped Dad to bake four honey cakes. Then they helped Grandpa set the table. Later, they ran into the garden with Mum. She lifted them on her shoulders, one at a time, so they could each pick an apple. Then the twins helped prepare the apple and honey. Ben arranged the apple slices on a plate while Amy spooned honey into a dish. As they were carrying them, they both tried to push through the door together. They almost dropped the

apple and honey on the floor! The twins looked upset and then very cross with one another.

'You can't feel cross at Rosh Hashana!' said Mum. 'Remember why we listen to the shofar!' The twins looked at one another, and smiled.

'Sorry!' they both said at the same time. Then Ben let Amy go first.

'Thank you, Ben,' she said.

That evening, everyone dipped their apple in the honey, and said 'Shana Tova! Happy New Year!'

Next day, they all walked to synagogue in their new clothes. Ben wore his new blue skullcap, just like Dad's and Grandpa's. At synagogue, they heard the shofar, which was very loud. Afterwards, they went to their cousins' house for another lovely meal and ate juicy pomegranates.

When the twins went back to school, they took lots of apples from their tree, and two jars of honey. At assembly time, they told everyone about Rosh Hashana. Then everyone joined in an action song called 'Is it Rosh Hashana?' and ate apple and honey. It was such good fun that, the next day, Amy and Ben wished it was Rosh Hashana all over again!

Linda Mort

Grow and move

When we are nought
We lie and kick our legs in the air.
When we are one
We crawl about here and there.
When we are two
We toddle and wobble.
When we are three
We run quite quickly!
When we are four
We can kick a ball across the floor.
And when we are five
We can dress ourselves!

Linda Mort

Shana Tova

(Sung to the tune of 'Twinkle, Twinkle, Little Star')

This is a wish for everyone to hear...
We hope we'll all have a happy new year!
This is what we want to say –
We hope we'll be happy
every day!
SHANA TOVA!

Linda Mort

Happy birthday, world!

(Sung to the tune of 'Happy Birthday')

Happy birthday to you,
Happy birthday to you,
Happy birthday, dear world,
Happy birthday to you!

We love the sun,
And the moon too,
We love the stars,
Yes we do!

We love the grass,
And the flowers too,
We love the trees,
Yes we do!

Linda Mort

Is it Rosh Hashana?

(Sung to the tune of 'I Hear Thunder')

It is winter *(Repeat)*
Let's build a snowman *(Repeat)*
Is it Rosh Hashana? *(Repeat)*
No, not yet! *(Repeat)*

It is summer *(Repeat)*
We swim in the sea *(Repeat)*
Is it Rosh Hashana? *(Repeat)*
No, not yet! *(Repeat)*

It is springtime *(Repeat)*
The blossoms float down *(Repeat)*
Is it Rosh Hashana? *(Repeat)*
No, not yet! *(Repeat)*

It is autumn *(Repeat)*
The leaves swirl round *(Repeat)*
Is it Rosh Hashana? *(Repeat)*
Yes, it is! *(Repeat)*

Linda Mort

Bees lap up nectar and fly away home
To make yummy honey in a honeycomb!
Let's all draw a honeycomb cell
Let's draw a hexagon very well!
1, 2, 3, 4, 5, 6!

Linda Mort

(The children count as they 'draw' the sides in the air with their fingertips.)

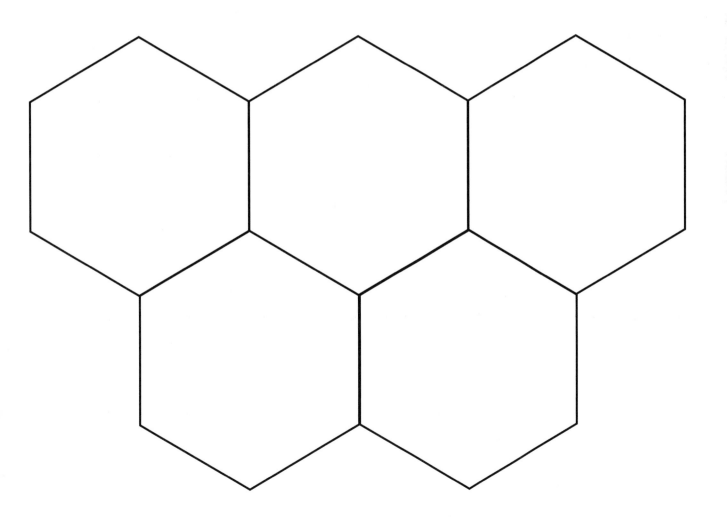

Sounds	People

For front of card

Shana Tova
Happy New Year

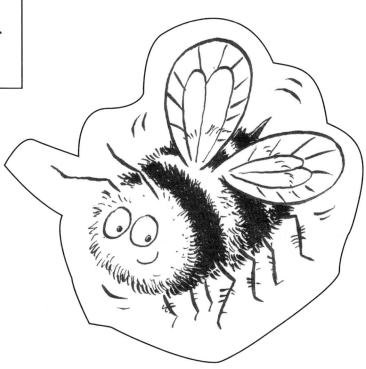

For inside card

שנה טובה

Love from

RESOURCES

Books for adults

A Different Light – the Hannukah Book of Celebration edited by Naom Zion and Barbara Spectre (Pitspopany Press)

Celebration – The Book of Jewish Festivals edited by Naomi Black (Jonathan David Publishers)

Festivals Around the World by Meryl Doney (*Discover Other Cultures* series, Franklin Watts)

Homing in – A Practical Resource For Religious Education in Primary Schools by Angela Wood (Trentham Books)

The Jewish Holiday Home Companion by Nicolas Mandelkern (Behrman House Publishing)

The Children's Book of Jewish Holidays by David A Adler (*Artscroll Youth* series, Artscroll)

All About Hanukkah by Judyth Groner (Kar-ben Copies Inc)

Hanukkah Fun – Great Things to Make and Do by Judy Bastyra (Kingfisher Books)

Jewish by Jenny Wood (*Our Culture* series, Franklin Watts)

Miracle Meals Cookbook – Eight Nights of Food 'n Fun for Chanukah by Madeline Wikler and Judyth Groner (Kar-ben Copies Inc)

Books for children

My Jewish Faith by Anne Clark (*Red Rainbows* series, Evans Brothers)

Hanukkah! A Three-Dimensional Celebration by Sara Freedland and Sue Clarke (Tango Books)

Hanukkah Oh Hanukkah! (Kar-ben Copies Inc)

Hanukkah Lights, Hanukkah Nights by Leslie Kimmelman (Harpercollins)

Like a Maccabee by Raymond A Zwerin (UAHC Press)

Sammy Spider's First Hanukkah by Sylvia Rouss (Kar-ben Copies Inc)

Sammy Spider's First Rosh Hashanah by Sylvia Rouss (Kar-ben Copies Inc)

Resource Packs

Judaism Photo Pack (Folens Publishers)

Festival Ideas Bank (Folens Publishers)

Equipment

Hanukkah candles; Hanukkah wall hanging; Festival of Light wall hanging; Happy Hanukkah House (3-D soft toy, consisting of house, Hanukiah, driedel, purse and Hanukkah 'gelt'); Hanukkah Temple (3-D soft toy, consisting of Temple and characters from the Hanukkah story) – all available from Articles of Faith Ltd, Resource House, Kay Street, Bury BL9 6BU, tel: 0161-763 6232, website: www.articlesoffaith.co.uk

Rosh Hashana cards (set); Shofar; Large Wooden Driedel (With Notes) – all available from Religion in Evidence (TTS), Nunn Brook Road, Huthwaite, Sutton-in-Ashfield, Nottinghamshire NG17 2HU, tel: 0800-318686, website: www.tts-shopping.com

Websites

www.jewishpeople.net/jewishholidays.html
www.myjewishlearning.com
www.theredirectory.org.uk
www.torah.org
www.joi.org/celebrate/rosh
www.totallyjewish.com

Organisations

Board of Deputies of British Jews, 6 Bloomsbury Square, London WC1A 2LP, tel: 020-7543 5400, website: www.bod.org.uk

Jewish Education Bureau, 8 Westcombe Avenue, Leeds LS8 2BS, tel: 0870-800 8532, website: www.jewisheducationbureau.co.uk

Reform Synagogues of Great Britain, The Sternberg Centre, 80 East End Road, London N3 2SY, tel: 020-8349 5640; website: www.reformjudaism.org.uk